Monologues of the consigliori

Kofi Essel-Appiah

BookLeaf
Publishing

Presentation by *BookLeaf Publishing*

Web: www.bookleafpub.com

E-mail: info@bookleafpub.com

ISBN: 978-93-95890-23-6

First edition 2022

PREFACE

Fear is an interesting thing,

something I have been almost ruminating
recently, and I thought

it an interesting topic to write and put thoughts
and ideas on paper. One of the main things

I find intriguing upon considering the concept is
the numerous layers that fear exists on.

If I and many other people decide to be honest,
most especially with ourselves, we can see

that fear is ….leaked out into psyche from so
many different places.

You can think right now, and probably name two
places or sources where you received a seed

of fear from. And those will only be the ones
that come to your mind .

Thinking, fear seems to come from the external
environment, experienced as something alien, an
outside force.

I think that is the deception in fear.

The truth is. It can only exist in the mind.

You have probably heard it:

Danger is real. Fear isn't.

And this was the rationalisation I had to go through to try this, and I hope this brings value to whoever reads this as well.

Preliminary prologue -

Oh the days of plenty, prosperity and power,

these truly test me,

for they are one messenger that whispers of the
imminence of darkness lurking ,

and of the pursuing of the plague of pride,
which endangers ,

Yet the irony ,

during the dark depths of the dusk,

where the trying and testing of thriving, is life.
live

is where I am showered with the most assurance
of the ability to overcome

,and inner peace abounds

in the knowledge,

of the dawning of a new day,

humility is ones solace.

My piece to a placement,

Please. pardon my paradox.

- consigliori.

the Photograph

CLICK.

Doubt, out
I wish to capture a picture,

Pressing the button and posing too,

Could you show me how?

Who

would be able to take the task,

I wonder if I need
 speed,
 focus,
 stillness,
Persistence,
patience,

I had a straw hat, and line

Under the sun, with a hatchet and a gun,

Seeds in my hand, and some time, trying to have
fun.

- consigliori.

Kill the boy.

Reality creeps, socks on feet,

The abyss calls,
how many feet?

How many
 took this fall,
kilometers for all

Weight rested on my shoulders

And the rest of me trying to stand tall.

Damn deep dives into my recesses,

Past the reef of my weaknesses,

Beyond the trench of my teetering on the edge of
excess. Is.

The struggle.

Drown the boy. Suffocated in fear.
We all will miss him.

But I need to get back.
Left the man at the peer.

- consigliori.

The Secret War

fire did blaze in my irises,

creating an automatic scorn and wish to create
great burning,

Despair turned to loathing and contempt,

A fierce and bloody battle tween rage and
pacification,

reason,
a sly devil player of both sides,

eventually to its timely demise,

1st instinct and 2nd guesses supplying arms.

Rain of emotion flooding the perception farms.

strangers and foreigners, the new allies,

the old familiar faces, turned enemies,

at last

the final deafening silence sounded loudly,

signaling the end of the murderous skirmish:

Pain : the menued dish, avec confusion

Description : a vicious battle where nobody
won.

- consigliori.

1 am on a week night

Blinds drawn like the red sea parted
Reveal the mystery
When the light shines through
Away casting said dark,
Starkly will.
Cut through, smoothly, like a hot knife
And butter cutter :

My eyes are heavy,
When my brain is ready , behind the windows
reddy
Oxymoronic paradox,
I'm well versed in literaturology,
not a word
But that's tautology
I admire these beautiful mistakes,
A claim I have staked
to those misses,
Beautifully chancing on fate
where I received my certificate,
in a
school of hard knocks,
And a gown and cap made with locks.

So simple:
to graduate I had to open up the doors,

I still shine my windows,

 so I can
Shatter the glass ceilings then destroy the marble
floors
Then live off the land with a tropical view,
Somewhere offshore.

----

3 times out of 4, left out the need to settle the
score,
Yet still deep search within the depths of the
vessel
Finally found the spots to go for the ores,
Oars rowing through
Oceans deeper in red,
Oceans in blue.

Okay now we begin.

Longer the wait to win,
in a different space for men,
In a different space or 20
Different spaces
And untied laces on a twisting road,

The creating:
Both a journey and an abode.

- consigliori.

VIEWS

I sit, I sit, I dangle legs,
I toe and point, I swivel and turn
I see and view, I perceive then learn,

What a surreal moment, this pause in time,
These...characters slow moving, silent, and
mimes,
These valleys and mountains, rises and falls,
time speeds and time stalls,
These views, the drink life brewed, sits on my
table, bubbling and unstable,
...these theses, thesis, is that I'm
thinking..troubled thoughts, deep in mental
travel with the hope of not tripping,

Views, Witness my landscape, a tragic comedy,
or comedic tragedy, no escape for this
scapegoat,...
thinking of something to do with soup and
float....

The mind is a bit hazy,
 I guess The thought escaped me..

But look who's caught,

it's me,
in a mental cot: the infant elder,

maybe I'm not caught, I'm cat, twirled in a life
twine,

and then I can't find the words because I got

stuck between the lines...

Views, its the end of seeing,
believing takes the spotlight,

if I could perceive,
 then
perhaps I could spot the light,

at the end of my tunnel,
before I emerge,
 surge in awareness of my 7th sense,
and then I sit,
or stand up before I fall,

I point, down travels the gavel

the story is unraveled,

the eyes open,
 views : the landscape is revealed,

the entrance unsealed
...behold:
 the views.
- consigliori.

Insomnia

Nothing

Right to write.

Right to write.

Wrote.

I love to quote.

Gems.

Broken

of from the stems,

with seeds

Weed out the weeds, musical chairs and poetic
wells I bleed.

I lay down. With a smiled frown.
Talk less. Listen more.

Lowkey Odd how you add less to even the score. Simple mathematics.

Multiply and conquer..

Was the saying I remember

The rest comes through after rest.

- consigliori.

the ending bell

People
 seep into our cracks, as a rushing flow over a
gutter, slippery as melted butter, check the
energy,
Synergy, necessary, definitely,to nurture a noble,
royal,
into a worker, usurped,
Of the very throne possessed, who's to say if
they are?
Spirits dipping and diving In-between, only
thing seen, is a flash of light, glow, or sheen,
speeds similar to a throwing stone,
Is our nature, nature? Or even nature's nature?
And who nurtures? Or nay. Not nurture..a
digression.
In the same way, digression from our future
path, pertaining from poor perception of the
past, with plagiarised present as a an unfit yet
sole present to a pair of generations that will be
put in a possibly perilous place.
Don't pause at the starting bell.
It's playtime.
Protect yourself at all times.

- consigliori.

conquest pages

Vien ici,
May those who struggle,
garner the right, to utter
Veni vidi vici, hindsight: 20/20 vision,
Behind the fight,
in each soul, majestic missions,
With surgical incisions into rich and turmoil
fueled heritage,
And heavenbound cultural emissions from a
slow burning rage,
Aromatic with that bittersweet scent,
mm..traumatic sage.
Macroscopic; the view of division,
Microscopic relational contusions
Yet still the royalty remains in the culture,
And yet still
the royalty remains in the realm of the blood,
monarch DNA deep in each neighbourhood

Vidi , yonder lies the light, bright yet faint at the
end of the journey,
Though dark was the stone that the builder
thought he would refuse, yet still appreciation
would return and lead to the brick reused,

the cornerstone : representation of the people:
the muse.

Vici.
won victory
within an ongoing battle bloody,
from unbroken spirit within the sometimes
broken body..
Yet still there is triumph…
..success story to be revealed shortly.

- consigliori.

Days of the best

Days of the best
but days that put me to the test,
With bulletproof vests to weather rain-showers
Of existence,
And here,
lies my song of sixpence
I awake to my faith for porosity and absorption,
and cocooning,
This is the veld of velour,
Misty:
the hue of my couture,
and my prayer;
Vibrancy inside the Duller,

 And even there:
With the test of so much wahala,
I witness through Sisyphus formats even in
Valhalla,
My Hope is sandwiched between a barbecue of
trabaja,
marinated with the seasoning: Inshallah.

- consigliori.

Law and Literature

was feeling passive,

 passing through unfulfilling motion,

no passion, deep search for a muse, to make a
masterpiece,

music, trying to meet creation with inspiration,
the two being bitter brats,

stubborn and drastic-ally, irate at each other,
deliberate and dogged determination not to see
eye to eye,

a judge is needed at once.
where's appreciation? absent.

criticism shall take her place, to cater for the role
in the crucial case,

passiveness held in contempt of court,
passion
being the witness and the evidence and the
lawyer
that concluded the matter.

peace the judge at last,
inner too, so that the two may be united as one
and move to give birth to THIS.

- consigliori.

mess

Quick , the tick of the clock,
like the ship at the dock,
click of the lock, the end to the story ,

Till the slow,
cool: the flow,
river;
closed the door,

 the way we paid in full at the store,

we bring to you war,
Shift right,
with a slight,
nod ,
the rod,
long enough ,
like that leap of the toad,
Used to hit the road,
what a load,
to carry, it's a starry night ,
 the right to fight, to light the fire to the
explosion ,
A problem , an inquisition, a mission,
a wishing,

a twisting, turning, burning,
blood curdling , screaming,
teeming with psychosis,
growth is.

emerging and slowly surging ,
upward through the surface ,
Broken orafice ,

clear, tears , could not bare, the fear, despair, the
hurt,
Terrible , disgusting , filthy, the unbearable truth
about the situation was :
the cause and effect, that in the middle could not
be dissected, or directed , was in reality :
Nothing less,
And nothing more than ;
a mess.

-

not a poem

This is not a poem,

It's a show, showing, glowing, throwing light on
to the long path,
journey,
through the wilderness and through the
meadows,
on top of the mountains and in the craters
so rigorous and simple.
A deadlift of a conjoining of heart and mind,
spirit and soul,
This is not a poem,
this a never ending
demonstration of a struggle and triumph,
knowledge, deception and wisdom ,
what a feeling,
a fowl depositing an empty shell ,
a facade, mirage.
On the other side stands the shadow
and broken reflection
with accusations of fraud and deception.
But this is not a poem.
It is a mural of the thoughts
 of one who is on a great quest of searching,
wandering,

looking for a point
equipped with no map
and a compass,
what a medley.
This is not a poem,
this is a winding road
down to an empty chasm
at the end of which is an oasis
 isolated from all.

Land ho.

- consigliori.

The Cold Wars

Responding, he (brain) said down the hallway,
through the bathroom doors, on the right,
That is. The location of the lab,

So large yet capacity has always remained the
singular staff,

The turnover rate, similar to the numbers of
those attempting attack,
 wait, no,
Much more like the total of the numbers of
fallen crates,
Don't rate these challenges.
It's bait.

Me cast away, eventually to be elected,
Same way I anticipated,
Expecting the unexpected,
Adversity should've done the same,
Something to do with a focus distance problem,
It becomes more difficult when your nose is
pressed against the frame

Because when the eyes were widened,
The field of vision remained unchanged.

- consigliori.

Fallacy

It was your burning desire
That stoked the fire.

The wanted conclusion that you loved to be
stated (illusion),
Fueling this enticing fantasy that your mind
inevitably created
With the day ended, conduct the disappointment,
somewhat an interesting investment.
As reality crescendos and crashes on the lie
This is the real mess, the one fated, and you
didn't know
That you orchestrated.

- consigliori.

Hunger and Flight.

Its inevitable, the unsatiable, unquenching, will
be mentioned, it's ventured forth, as an eruption
of empty unfulfilling motion, NO PROGRESS.
WHAT A MESS.
With jest, and joviality, forced until the blaring
stare of inauthenticity scorches, and parches, a
forever singing throat, that sways an unanchored
boat.

I find myself drowning and searching,
Gagged and hurting, till the illusion is
REVEALED, and the veil, shows and exposes,
Me : protagonist of this farce, yet still scarce-Ly,
as a cause for comedy, my story - a disfigured
melody
Rises as smoke, wafting in the wind,
Hope for no chokes,
an escape convict,
to fly with eagles.

- consigliori.

My search for beauty in boredom

My search for beauty in boredom
Longing to access the prior locked off intricate,
intriguing, exquisite world behind the virtual
Oh for the resolute power against the allure,
Temptations, that which pulls in only to obscure,

My speech into the future is that I come into
Understanding and
Connection
With
Time , in the way I attempt to connect and relate
with this rhyme.

Got bored searching beauty. Then found it. The
loop may now begin again.
The beginning and end, at the same part of this
line.

- consigliori.

Soundtrack to the militant maestro

These eyes, now more hollow than they once
were... Can no longer recognize,
These hands cracked and rough, struggle to
bear....no longer feel, fire or ice,
This mind, will it continue to wind and spiral,
chances left random as cards and dice,
I find myself in a strange place, an unfamiliar
maze, a local turned foreign,
A veteran recruit who has ended his start to
warring,
Only to begin writing:
 the musical manuscript to the chaos he's
scoring.

- consigliori.

attempted mutiny.

Close my eyes
And jump of the edge, my wish to fall
Forever, focus shift:
 from fear, to freedom.
Close my eyes and see all the faces,
Pulling wool over my eyes,
My windows may be blurred,
They keep getting misty after so many tries
To wipe the cries.
If I keep falling, I think i can submerge myself
in the tide.
Wash over me, clarity,
Watch over me. Public scrutiny.
You could spot it from a mile away. Anxiety
conspired the mutiny 😐.

In the case I do drown. I'll remain at peace.
I'll go on my own terms.
There was nothing you could do to me.

- consigliori.

W poem.

To question

What happens when you strip down all the unnecessary?

Stress, fear, anxiety ,

non essential makes wary,

And increase

      the weight

         mass on the scale. Cut the fat off the plate.

I think makes for better mental

     STATE.

\- consigliori.

doubt out.

A constant struggle, conflict with an
unforgiving...
Muddled
Choke holds disguised as snuggles,
cold shrugs,
masks the shivering whispers,
mind snickering,
With whispers of disloyalty not bickering,

Wrong right
We keep the tops peeled, knowing, searching
I kept my logs stilled, despite uncertain sowing,
Still hurting,
You will keep yourself willed, for the seed
growing..
Till the tree blooms and then we close the
curtain.

- consigliori.